One Summer
at Grandmother's House

Poupa. M

One Summer at Grandmother's House

by Poupa Montaufier
translated from the French by Tobi Tobias

Carolrhoda Books, Inc. / Minneapolis

This edition first published by Carolrhoda Books, Inc., 1985
Original edition first published by Éditions du Centurion, Paris, France,
1983 under the title UN ÉTÉ CHEZ GRAND-MÈRE
Copyright © 1983 Éditions du Centurion, Paris
English translation copyright © 1985 by Tobi Tobias

Manufactured in the United States of America

LIBRARY OF CONGRESS CATALOGING IN PUBLICATION DATA

Montaufier, Poupa.
    One summer at grandmother's house.

    Translation of: Un été chez grand-mère.
    Summary: A reminiscence about a French girl and her
family spending a typical summer with her grandmother
in Alsace.
    1. France—Social life and customs—20th century—
Juvenile literature. 2. Montaufier, Poupa—Juvenile
literature [1. Family life—France. 2. France—
Social life and customs] I. Title.
DC33.7.M6513 1985   944.083   85-3758
ISBN 0-87614-238-2 (lib. bdg.)

    2 3 4 5 6 7 8 9 10 94 93 92 91 90 89 88 87 86

Contents

One Summer
at Grandmother's House

We Arrive in Alsace

The sun is going down. The afternoon is almost over. In the car, my brother and I are restless. We've been driving for nine hours. We left Paris this morning. We are going to spend our summer vacation at Grandmother's in Alsace, the way we do every year.

To pass the time, Mother points out the sights along the road. The hopvines are in bloom, climbing up their tall poles. The apple trees don't belong to anyone in particular. People will gather the fruit and sell it at auction.

Finally, the main street of the village! The storks are back in their nest, their long legs folded up under them. I always wonder how they manage to fit such long legs into a nest.

And here is Grandmother's house! Aunt Margrite comes down the stairs as fast as she can. "Have you been here long?" she asks.

"We just got here," Mother says. "And we've seen the storks."

Aunt Margrite says, "There are even some babies in the village nest this year."

Aunt Margrite is Grandmother's cousin. She often thinks just the opposite of what everyone else is thinking. The family says she's an original.

She is always delighted to see us arrive. She's already imagining everything that will make these two summer months fun—battles between herself and Grandmother to convince us that one is always right and the other wrong. Meanwhile, she asks us lots of questions about our trip.

I raise my eyes anxiously toward the front stoop. Usually Grandmother rushes to greet us first, each time trying to get to the foot of the steps before Aunt Margrite does. What's happened?

Mother is worried too. "Where is Grandmother?" she asks. "Is she ill?"

Aunt Margrite shrugs her shoulders. "Of course not. She's in church. You know very well that the minute she hears the church bells, she can't keep still. She's off, her hat any which way, running to church."

The apples will be sold at auction in the fall

The House

Father gets the suitcases out of the car while Mother goes through the house to see if anything has changed since last year. "There was no point in having the shutters painted," she says. "They're no better than they were before."

Aunt Margrite lifts her eyes to the heavens. "You haven't seen anything yet."

While she's talking with Mother, I take the chance to slip away. Our cousin Richard is already hurrying my brother off to play in the garden. Richard always comes to stay with Grandmother in the summertime too. Two at a time, I climb the stairs; I'm going to find my secret world again. Yes, my room is just as I left it. There's the old bicycle frame against the wall, waiting for wheels. Piles of pillows and eiderdown quilts lie on the bed. Scattered on the floor are drawers filled with odd old things.

All the old familiar smells are there, too, especially the one of dried flowers. Reassured, I go slowly back downstairs.

Aunt Margrite has taken Father and Mother to the dining room. For a minute they're so surprised they can't say a word. Then they start to laugh.

"It's a wallpaper store!"

Each wall is covered with a different flowered paper.

Just at that moment, Grandmother arrives. She stands in the doorway, not moving. I hope she hasn't heard. I rush over to hug her.

I think she's beautiful, my grandmother, with her black shawl and her braided-straw hat. She's clutching her imitation-leather pocketbook, which always holds a nicely ironed handkerchief, an old prayer book with raggedy corners, and a coin for the collection plate.

She gives us an embarrassed look, then explains to Mother, "This way of wallpapering was the painter's idea. He told me it was very modern. Besides, I got a bargain."

"A bargain for him," Mother says, low. "He sold you his leftover bits and pieces."

Nothing has changed since last year

Oma's Four Aprons

We call my grandmother "Oma." Grandmothers are often called that in Alsace.

Early in the morning, after the first mass, Oma carefully puts her going-to-church outfit away in the big wooden armoire, which smells of wax and mothballs. Before she begins her housework, she covers her gray dress with a big apron. But that's not all. She always has to have three or four aprons. One is gathered and tied around her waist. Another has a bib. Finally there's the last—a washed-out black one, so worn it's almost in shreds.

"Tell me, Oma, why do you always wear that ugly black apron?"

"Little one, its purpose is not to be handsome, but to protect the others."

Aunt Margrite doesn't care for the way Oma is dressed either and doesn't hesitate to compare her, with all her layers, to an enormous winter onion. But Oma doesn't listen to anyone. She sticks to her own ways.

When she comes back from mass, she has her coffee alone in the kitchen, before anyone else is down. While she drinks it, she thinks about what she will give us to eat today. She enjoys her coffee and slowly dunks her bread in the big cup. Only Mitzelle, the cat, is allowed in the kitchen at this time. She laps her warmed milk, making her saucer clink on the tile floor.

Next, Oma goes to the hen coop, wrapped in her four aprons. "The hens always recognize me," she says.

The hen coop, a few steps away from the house, is a fenced-in place, partly overgrown with nettles. Here and there, the cheeping birds' red crests pop up out of the nettles, like walking poppies. There are a dozen half-wild birds there, who rush to the gate as soon as Oma appears with her pail of feed. I follow her at a distance. I don't dare get too near the birds or the nettles. One scares me as much as the other.

Each morning Oma goes out to feed her chickens

One Match Too Many

We've only just finished breakfast, but Grandmother is already asking Mother, "What shall we make for dinner?"

Every morning it's the same story. Mother answers without any enthusiasm. "How can I think about it at this hour? I've hardly gotten up from the table."

Finally Mother suggests a menu, which, of course, doesn't suit Oma. Oma already has her own ideas. So there's Mother with a pile of vegetables to clean. The soup must be started early; it has to simmer for a long time.

Curious as weasels, Aunt Margrite and Oma keep an eye on Mother to see if she's kept their good, thrifty habits. Oma bustles back and forth. She adds a piece of wood to the stove, listens for the noises in the street. Actually, she's waiting for the moment when Mother will put the big pot on the gas ring. It must come to a boil there before it goes on the stove to simmer.

The minute Mother reaches for the box of matches, there is Oma protesting, "Oh, no, you're not going to use a match when we have such a good fire."

Oma rushes toward the stove, waving a sheet of loosely rolled-up newspaper, which she sticks into the fire. She takes giant steps across the kitchen, her flaming torch in hand, to light the gas. Each time, Aunt Margrite is sure that her cousin is going to set fire to the house. But Oma says that small savings make great riches. With one hand she opens the gas tap; with the other she slides her newspaper torch under the pot, which gets all black. Aunt Margrite walks away, making a little face of disgust. Mother sighs and says nothing.

She doesn't even say anything when Oma disconnects the refrigerator several times a day. Grandmother's excuse? "These modern appliances cost money to run, and it's cold enough like that."

Small savings make great riches

The Lost Spectacles

The vegetables are simmering on the stove. Drops of water escape from under the cover of the pot and burst with a dry sound as they hit the metal stove top.

Settled in an armchair near the window, Aunt Margrite is embroidering. She tells me stories about when she was little, and I sit at her feet on a low stool, listening. Aunt Margrite has traveled and knows lots of things. I never get tired of asking her questions.

Suddenly—what's happening? Oma is upset. She cries, "Where can they have gotten to?"

Aunt Margrite gives a discontented sigh. "You've lost your spectacles again."

Still, she gets up to help her cousin look for them. She knows that Grandmother can't do without her spectacles, though they are old and bent and patched up with tape.

"I don't understand," says Oma. "They were here five minutes ago."

She then casts a suspicious glance after my brother, who has wisely disappeared into the garden.

In the afternoon, we help Oma hoe the garden, pick tomatoes, and gather the plums that have fallen from the tree. She really can't see very well. At dinner time, still no spectacles. Oma brings the big tin pot to the table, holding it with two red crocheted potholders to protect her hands. I smell something strange.

"That smells funny, Oma."

"Quiet," says Aunt Margrite. "Children should not talk at the table."

Oma begins to serve the soup. But suddenly she stops. She is looking at her spectacles, which dangle sadly from the serving spoon, twined with leek leaves. Oma blushes with embarrassment. She grabs the sticky spectacles and runs into the kitchen to rinse them off under the tap.

She comes back, turning them in all directions, with a contented expression. "Notice," she says, "how well they survived being cooked."

Oma carries in the large pot of soup

Baking Day

Today, like every Saturday, is baking day at our house, as it is all over the village. I come down the stairs, happy to be with Oma and Aunt Margrite in the kitchen. Oma is already enthusiastically kneading the stretchy dough. I can't resist stealing a few lumps of baker's yeast. Ugh! It's awful, and besides, it sticks to the roof of your mouth like cement. One last pat and Oma turns the dough into an enameled bowl, which she covers with a clean towel.

A few hours later, she slowly lifts the bulging cloth, and we marvel at the beautiful white dome that has risen up underneath.

"Hand me the big pastry board," says Aunt Margrite.

She flours the thick wooden board well. Now it's time to choose the molds from the buffet where they have been piled up helter-skelter since my great-grandmother's time. Oma always takes the same ones. They are never washed, never cleaned off, because the molds last longer that way.

I kneel on a chair, resting my chin in my hands. Oma cuts the white dome into quarters. The dough parts as the knife slides through it, giving off a delicious smell of yeast. Then she flattens each part with a rolling pin and sets it into the fluted molds.

Aunt Margrite sits down in the best dining-room chair and begins to arrange the fruit like an artist. She leans her head forward a little and scrunches up her eyes. Each tart will be different from the others. Oma pits the fruit quickly, and I taste the peaches without paying any attention to what they say.

Aunt Margrite gives her work an approving look: the juicy yellow plums speckled with brown, the purple and blue plums set out in curves or triangles, according to her fancy. Once again this week, she has invented new designs! Satisfied, she gets up, catching up the corners of her apron, which holds a hoard of delicious crumbs for the birds.

Aunt Margrite arranges the fruit like an artist

The Bakery

Oma runs to the little shed to get the wicker cart that she uses to carry tarts to the baker's big oven. Out on the main street, we meet our neighbors, who are also pushing their tart-filled carts.

At the bakery, we carefully unload our treasures, and the baker's wife labels them with our name. We return home, dragging the empty cart behind us. Now we just have to wait.

Toward the end of the day, we go to pick up our baked pastries. Oma stacks the burning-hot tarts on the little cart, careful to keep them balanced. Smiling, Aunt Margrite comes toward us, eager to admire her work. And what do you know? In the midst of all those beautiful golden suns, she discovers an ugly, flat, grayish cake, speckled with oats.

"What is that awful thing?" exclaims my aunt furiously.

"Oh dear, and I didn't even notice," Grandmother adds, shocked.

Together they dash off to the bakery to demand an explanation. I run after them, leaving the cart right in the middle of the street; I'm dying to see what will happen. The baker is standing in front of his shop, arms folded, chatting peacefully with a customer. Oma and Aunt Margrite pour a stream of questions and reproaches over him. The baker frowns, then he begins to laugh. He explains, "You know Marie Diestel, the old maid who lives in the lane behind the church? Well, every Saturday she brings a cake to be baked for her horse, Teiffel. The poor lady doesn't get along with anyone, and he is her only friend."

"For her horse!" Aunt Margrite repeats, astonished. I can hardly keep from laughing.

Aunt Margrite and Oma go on their way, with plenty to say about this unexpected turn of events.

Everyone brings their tarts to the baker's for baking

The Village Festival

The last Saturday in August is the village festival. For this important day, Oma has left her dreary aprons hung up on a nail. She is wearing a pretty black dress decorated with little jet buttons. Her hair is neatly combed back into a chignon that twines around and around like a snail's shell.

The whole family is out on the terrace to see the parade of recruits—the boys who are going off to do their army service. Oma adjusts her spectacles. She is amazed.

"Look, that's one of the Loux boys. I didn't think they had a son that age."

Aunt Margrite, with her expert eye, is in ecstasy over the round aprons embroidered by the boys' fiancées, according to an old Alsatian custom. The recruits jump and dance to a tune played on the accordion. Now the recruits from nearby villages arrive in charabancs. Everyone claps enthusiastically. My heart pounding with excitement, I run off as fast as I can to join a bunch of children.

The recruits stop at the village inn. The owner greets them with a smile and offers them a glass of beer. We children aren't allowed inside. Seated on the steps of the inn, we hear laughing and the clatter of heels. More curious than the others, I hoist myself up to the window, clinging to the edge of the sill. Fascinated, I see—between two geraniums—the recruits dancing. The magnificent felt hats they have borrowed from their fathers are trimmed with multicolored ribbons that flutter with every movement.

Ugh! Before I know what's happening, I find myself doused with a glass of brownish beer. Sputtering and ashamed, with everyone laughing at me, I take off for the safety of my family.

Oma storms, "Where have you been? Will you look at this fool?"

Without any warning, she grabs me with one hand, and with the other she lays hold of the wicker carpet beater and—*Whut!* She can really hurt.

She's not mean. She just thinks that that's how you make children behave.

The recruits parade down the main street of the village

The Afternoon in the Attic

The weather is stormy this afternoon. With nothing to do, my brother and I wander around the house for a while. Cousin Richard joins us, and we decide to go up to the attic.

In the storeroom, the sight of the pillows and eiderdown quilts gives us an idea. My brother throws a pillow at Richard, who throws one back. I try to join in, but the weight of a quilt makes me clumsy, and, *Crack!* The material of the quilt cover tears under my foot. Out from the rip, a cloud of goose feathers flies up toward the ceiling. The feathers fall gently down again, changing the three of us into snowmen.

Aunt Margrite hears us laughing and shouting and rushes into the room. To our great surprise, she goes out again, closing the door without a word. What punishment is she preparing for us? We wait nervously. But after a while, the boys get restless.

"What should we do?" Richard asks.

"Go down, what else?" my brother answers.

But Aunt Margrite has not forgotten our mischief. She is waiting for us by the attic door. She has her arms around a small mountain of potatoes, which she clasps to her bosom, and bombards us with them angrily.

Bang! Bang! Bang! The potatoes hit the wall and bounce back on the steps without hitting us. We run away, shrieking, not knowing how it will all end.

"Why on earth are you throwing potatoes around?" shouts Oma from the foot of the staircase.

"You'd better come and admire the work of your little angels. Where are you, anyway? Probably busy collecting horse manure in the street," screams our furious aunt.

"Now, now," Oma answers calmly. "It makes good fertilizer. You know you wouldn't be happy unless we had the best geraniums in the neighborhood."

Good! There they are, quarreling. This diversion comes in the nick of time to save us from a good spanking. And they go on arguing all the time they're trying to put the cloud of feathers back into its worn-out cover.

A cloud of goose feathers flies up toward the ceiling

Bedtime

It's already dark when the clock strikes nine with an insistence I don't like. I know. It is time for bed.

Tonight Oma wants me to sleep in her room. Most of the time she doesn't let me. She says that little girls are better off in their own beds, even if they are afraid of the dark.

I'm all excited by this unexpected chance. I hurry and put on my pink cotton nightgown and slide happily into Oma's bed with its big quilt divided into squares.

I hear Oma downstairs, crossing the kitchen to check the other doors. The front door is in a bad way; the rusty lock needs changing. But Oma has her own trick to take the place of the bolt. Every night, she drags out an old zinc dishwashing pan from the end of the tiled hall. It's filled with three quarts of rainwater that has turned green because she never changes it. This pan is used to hold the front door shut for the night. What a racket! I cover my ears.

When she's finished her tour of the house, Oma carefully lays out her clothes for morning mass. Every night she does exactly the same things in exactly the same way. Then, with all the lights out, she kneels down at her prie-dieu. Now and then little whisperings reach my ears. Then she slowly gets undressed, still absorbed in her prayers. I listen to the rustling of the material. I know that she is going to put on her heavy linen nightgown and join me. Finally, she sits on the edge of the bed and takes the hairpins out of her chignon with a sigh of relief. "Comb my hair," she says to me. "That does me good."

While I brush her long hair, she tells me a story. After a while, she takes the brush back, twists up her hair, and we both slide under the quilt.

"Ssh now," she says, "it's time to sleep."

I sink my head into the soft pillow. Tonight I'm not afraid of the dark.

Grandmothers must surely have secrets

The End of the Vacation

One day at the end of August, Oma says, "Marthe Kappler told me that the storks are gone."

This news dismays us. Once the storks have flown away, it means that we'll be leaving soon, too.

On the last day, Mother bustles all over the house, while I pack my little suitcase in my room. With my heart full, I look for treasures to take away with me.

We load up the car. Father starts to get annoyed.

"Do you really think we need all these packages?"

At the last minute, Oma runs to her room. It's pretty dark in there with the shutters closed. She opens the armoire, where she keeps a row of bottles of holy water perfectly lined up. Each one is labeled with the year it was brought back from a pilgrimage to Lourdes. At the back of the shelves, next to the holy water, Oma sets bottles of home-made brandy and jars of jam. She makes up a huge package, wrapped in newspaper, which she gives to my father with a commanding gesture.

"Take this brandy," she says. "You won't find anything like it in Paris."

Before we get on the road to Paris, we drop Cousin Richard off at the train station. I am fascinated by the enormous black steam engine that will take him to Strasbourg where his mother and father will pick him up.

At noon, we stop to picnic in the shade of a hop field. To help out, I take hold of a bottle, but it slips between my fingers and breaks with a dry thump. Petrified, I look at the crumpled newspaper left in my hand. It's Oma's brandy that's spilled all over the grass. Mother cries out. She is very annoyed. My father leans over.

"But there's no smell," he says. "It's only water!"

"What do you mean, water?" says Mother, getting all huffy.

Then I notice the label on the bottle. It's the one the priest brought Oma this summer from his pilgrimage to Lourdes.

The huge steam engine takes Cousin Richard away

About the Author

Poupa Montaufier was born in Alsace in 1944 and studied painting at the Beaux-Arts de Rouen. When Oma, her beloved Alsatian grandmother, died in 1976, Ms. Montaufier wanted to rediscover her own memories of past summers in Alsace and to "retain a clear memory of lovely customs in the hearts" of young and old alike. She then painted the exquisite scenes that were to become the illustrations for this authentic look at the charms and rigors of Alsatian village life in the 1950s.

Ms. Montaufier currently lives in Tonnay-Charente, France. Her favorite hobbies include cooking (she is especially good at baking Alsatian pies and tarts) and spending two days each week in Paris attending museums and exhibitions. The rest of her time she balances between writing and illustrating children's books, painting (her works have been exhibited in several French cities), and family life with her husband and three sons.

One Summer at Grandmother's House will inspire readers of all ages to remember the treasure-filled attics, warm fragrant kitchens, holidays, and special people locked in their own memories.